How You Like Me Now?

Clayborne Brown, Jr.

How You Like Me Now?

Clayborne Brown, Jr.

MILLIGAN BOOKS, INC.   BOOKS   CALIFORNIA

Printed and Bound in the United States of America
Published by:
Milligan Books

Cover Layout by K. Borne
Formatted by Milligan Books

First Printing May 2008

ISBN: 978-0-9815783-2-3

Milligan Books
1425 W. Manchester Blvd., Suite C
Los Angeles, CA 90047
www.milliganbooks.com
drrosie@aol.com
(323) 750-3592

This book is dedicated to anyone who may be doing drugs, whatever their drug of choice may be, and my deepest prayer is that this book might be an inspiration for them to get some help before it is too late. This book is also dedicated to anyone that has been chosen to do something and you know you have been chosen ... by all means, do it, because, "Today well lived makes yesterday a dream of happiness and tomorrow a vision of hope."

Acknowledgments

To GOD I GIVE ALL the praise, honor, and glory, because when I needed Him, He was there:

- ⚜ 1970—head injury, brain damage
- ⚜ 1975 & 1976—right knee surgery, could have lost leg
- ⚜ 1995—open heart surgery ... He is still with me today.
- ⚜ A special family that is very close to my heart—Debra Ecung and her husband, Ernest Ecung, Sr.—helped me get into the Open Door Mission Drug Program.
- ⚜ Ernest Ecung, II, and Eric Ecung—were there when I needed moral support, and they are still in my corner today.
- ⚜ Annie B. Davis—my big sister in Christ.

Contents

About The Author

CLAYBORNE BROWN, JR. AKA "MR. CLAY"

*B*ORN ON SEPTEMBER 1, 1952, in Houston, Texas, with a natural gift from God to write poetry and cook (he excels in both).

The author moved to Los Angeles, California, in September of 2000. He attends Calvary Baptist Church, L.A., under the leadership of Rev. Virgil V. Jones. For the past seven years he has been a faithful member of Calvary and was the sound technician for a few years. Mr. Clay has a God-given gift for helping people, which has made him an excellent caregiver. His cooking, caregiving, and writing poetry comes from the heart with great care.

Without going too deep into my past life, I used drugs—crack cocaine was my drug of choice. I thank God that I have been clean and sober eleven-plus years. October 26, 2008, will be twelve years. One day when I was at work, my employer told me she knew I was doing drugs and wanted to assist me in getting some help. Even though I told her I was not using or doing drugs, I asked her if I could take a rain check on her offer on one condition. She said, "Yes, and what is the condition?" My response was, "Should I come to realize that I do have a problem with drugs, can I come back and accept your offer?" and she said yes. I completed my work, fixed a lunch to take with me, got paid, and left.

Three days later, I called her and asked if her offer was still on the table. She said it was and told me to come over to the house and she would find a place for me to go to get help.

When I left her house and before I went to work at my regular job, I got high. (I was working for a dry cleaner on a shirt press.) I got hungry and tried to eat some chicken and rice, but could not, because it tasted like crack cocaine. I took a bite out of an oatmeal cookie, but could not eat it, because it tasted like crack cocaine. I got a peppermint candy, tasted it, and it tasted like crack cocaine. I even tried to drink some water, but could not, because it tasted like crack cocaine. I knew then that was God at work, because four different things all tasted like one (crack cocaine). God allowed me to see my reflection on a grey brick wall as if I were looking in a mirror. When I spoke, my upper lip went one way and my bottom lip went the opposite.

My equilibrium was off balance. When I took one step forward and my foot came down, it was three steps to the right or left of me. Somehow I ended up at the Open Door Mission. I graduated October 26, 1996, and the rest is history.

Look at me ... a living testimony.

My Testimony

*A*T ONE TIME IN MY life (March 1994), I was at the Open Door Mission with a drug problem. After being in the facility for several months, a urine analysis was done on me. I tested positive ... and I was asked to leave. I had gone to some of their meetings, like the Bible studies, but I never really worked the "twelve steps" (I only read them). But I did write poetry and it was an inspiration to others. Upon leaving the Open Door Mission at that time, I returned to the people that sought help for me in the beginning. I even became the live-in person at their home. My duties were to cook for the family, care for the two boys, wash, iron, etc. I never went to any meetings, but I did visit several churches until I found Jordan Grove. I enjoyed the services and joined.

During the two years I was with this family ... trust me, there was a lot of stress and pressure. Lo and behold, one day while entertaining an idle mind, Satan planted a thought and I acted upon that thought. Yes, I relapsed on April 22, 1996, but you know what? God is really good, because when I was smoking, a thought came into my head: "Keep one dollar and go to the

Open Door Mission," and I did. On April 23, 1996, I talked to Mike Naylor and signed a six-month agreement obligating myself to God. For the first two weeks, I was worried about where I would go or even be after the six months was over. I then remembered the saying, "Let Go and Let God." So one day while playing a tape, God showed me that I was looking at a snapshot instead of the big picture. It was then that I decided to leave it all in God's hands. Now, thanks be to God, I began to work and understand the twelve steps better. I now have a better relationship with God and through God's grace working in Mike Naylor, I am now more involved in the Bible so that God's light in me may be seen by others.

At this time in my life and program, I am more open-minded about things. I'm talking more, and I love sharing about what God has done for me to other people. Yes, ever since I truly let go to God, He has really inspired me because I now know that I am on God's time, doing His will. Yes, I do know it to be true; therefore, I thank God for the Open Door Mission, for Mike Naylor, and all my brothers in Christ here at the Open Door Mission.

Thank You Very Much
And remember: God loves you, and so do I.
Clayborne Brown, Jr.
October 10, 1996

At The Mission

I thank God for blessing me to see another sober day

And I thank Him for sending more men the Open Door
Mission way

The program here is not very hard; it is simple and easy to do

With God's help, it is working daily and successfully too

We do not offer silver or gold, but we do have peace and joy
in the Lord

Receiving blessings daily and living sober is our reward

We work the Twelve Steps, study God's Word, and share the
Holy Spirit every day

Because Jesus is the light, and He shows us the right way

Even though we have no roses here topped with the morning
dew

Trust me ... the Lord is here with a miracle waiting just for
you

Now that you are here ... thank God for giving you another
break

Because the gifts from God above are yours to freely take

—Welcome to the Open Door Mission

4/15/90

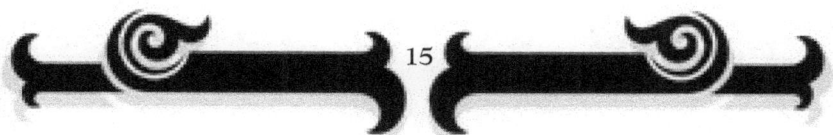

Did You Know?

It is one thing to read the Bible through and through
Another to read, to learn, and to do
Some read it as their duty once a week
But no instructions from the Bible do they seek
Some read to bring themselves into repute
By showing others how they can dispute
There are those who read it because their neighbors do
To see how long it will take them to read it through
Some read it for the wonders that are there
How David killed a lion and a bear
One may read with daddy glasses on his head
And see things just like his daddy said
Others read it with uncommon care
Hoping to find some contradictions there

DID YOU KNOW? ...

Some people read the Bible to prove a pre-adopted creed
Yet they understand very little of what they read
Even though there are many people who read the Bible right
There are still some who read it out of spite
So read the Bible prayfully and you will see
Whatever is right God's word will agree
... Because of what the early Bible prophets wrote
We find that Christ and His apostles quote
So trust no creed that troubles you to recall
What has been penned by one, and verified by all

3/4/93

Someone Special

Although it cannot be said in just a word or two
I now write a special poem for you
My feelings for you get stronger and stronger by the day
So here is what my heart has to say
… I would love to share with you the very best of myself
Because I really like you and no one else
Just knowing you makes it more worthwhile for me to live
Therefore, I will never ask of you no more than you can give
I like you for the little things you do constantly
Especially the unexpected things you have done for me
In your own way you have shown how much you care
Yet, your time, love, and affection I would love to share
… there is no way that I can resist
Your warm support, tender touch, and your sweet gentleness
… You are thought of daily in a godly way
And it is those thoughts that fill my lonely day
I ask myself, can this really be true
How someone can make me feel the way you do
To you I will never bring any harm
Because I love to caress and hold you deep in my arm
For you are so dear, so sweet, and someone special to me
And I thank God for each day He blesses us to see

4/8/93

The Store

Even tho' we live in a world full of misery and strife, I truly thank God for being a big part in my life ... I was riding down one of life's highways not so long ago, a sign caught my eye and it read, "The Store." I slowed down. As I got closer, the door opened very wide. Before I knew it, I was standing inside. I saw a band of angels standing everywhere. One gave me a basket and told me to shop with care. Everything a Christian needed was there in the store; all you could not carry you could always go back for more.

I knew what I needed for each day and everywhere I might go, so I started by getting some patience and love that was on the next row. I got a box or two of wisdom and a bag or two of faith. There was no way I could miss the Holy Ghost, because it was all over the place. I remembered to get some strength and courage to help me run this race. By that time, my basket was getting full, but I had room for some grace. I did not forget salvation, because salvation was free, so I tried to get enough to save you and me.

When I went to the counter to pay my bill, I knew—I had everything to do the Master's will. I walked down the aisle and I saw a line of prayers, so I put some in, because as soon as I walked outside, I would be walking back into sin. Peace and joy were plentiful, and they were on the last shelf. Song and praise were hanging around, so I just helped myself.

I asked the angels how much do I owe? They smiled and said, "Take them, everywhere you go." Again, I smiled at them and said, "How much do I really owe?" They smiled again and said, "My child, Jesus paid your bill a long time ago."

—Author Unknown

6/6/93

Blessed

*God has blessed me to share another poem. Even though it may
     be short*

Listen closely, take it dearly, and take it to heart

I woke up this morning, I heard the birds singing in harmony

I knew God gives life, and He blesses everything

Including you and me

Now let us give God thanks for blessing us to see another day

*Because today is special, and you, too, have a blessing coming
     your way*

So let us be happy, not sad, and may there be no inner strife

Accept God's will as you travel this road in life

Yes, I know God has really been good to me

And His blessings I can truly see

3/23/94

God Is

As we travel up and down life's road,
it may seem to be very hard
It really isn't if you believe and trust in God
Even though there may be things we may not understand
Fear not, fret not, because God has the master plan
God is the only one who blesses us from day to day
And I have learned to abide by and do as He says
God is the one who really cares for you
Because He is always there to see you through
Yes … He knows our hearts, our minds, and our every step
And He is always there when we need His help

4/1/94

A Special Man

We were made in the image of God—that we have in
   common
Yet, there was a man born the child of a peasant wom-
   an
He worked in a carpenter's shop and lived until He was
   thirty and three years
As He walked the earth, what He said and did was dear
Even though He preached and taught He brought no
   one any harm
And He never traveled more than 200 miles from where
   He was born
As a young man people turned against Him, and His
   friends ran away
The cock crowed three times … the man who denied
   Him had nothing to say
He carried His cross … many watched as He passed by
His mother was there filled with sorrow and did not cry
The place of His execution was on a hill just outside the
   city

As He hung, four soldiers gambled at His feet, having
    no pity
His cross was driven deep within the ground
After His death new life and salvation would be found
As He hung and bled He spoke to His Father and He
    did hear
He refused to drink of the bitter cup, so His senses may
    be clear
He was crucified between two thieves, according to
    prophecy
For the sins of this world, including you and me

He rose on the third day with all power in His hand

Because He did the will of His Father … making Him …

Jesus … a special man

4/2/94

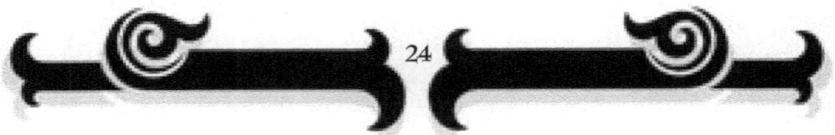

This Prayer

O heavenly Father, open our eyes so we may see
The love, mercy, and grace that comes from Thee
Even though You have the patience to tolerate us as we sin
  today
Through morning devotion and acceptance, I have learned to
  do as you say
I pray that You will fill my soul with a love so divine
It will make my heart to be more like Thine
Motivate me, dear Lord, each and every day
Be my strength as I live ... being aware of what I say
You are there when I'm reading and even when I'm talking
Please be the driver as I ride and when I'm walking
I pray this prayer daily as I walk with Thee
That ... more like Jesus ... I may one day be.
—Amen

4/9/94

Look At Me

Take a look at me … I made a mistake
With God's help I will make a comeback for my sake
… I took a step in the wrong direction
When I leave the mission, I will be striving for perfection
God will be the only leader in my life
Because I know He will handle all my strife
I made a mistake … we know that to be true
I will make a comeback … I know God will see me through
To know that Jesus is with me daily as time goes by
I will walk tall, and I will hold my head up high
… I know nothing in life is free
… I made a comeback, and I am as happy as can be
With the experiences I have had I know what to do
I keep my hand in the Master's hand, because He brought me
through
Now I walk a new path and everyone can see
I made a comeback, I have a new life, and I know Jesus still
walks with me

4/13/94

Please Tell Someone

My friend, I stand in judgment now
And I feel that you are the blame somehow
We walked together on earth day by day
… Never did you point or show me the way
You knew the Lord in truth and in glory
But you never told me the story

Even though my knowledge was very dim
You could have led me safe to Him
Yes, we lived together down on earth
And you never told me about the second birth
You taught me many things, this is true
Yet, I called you friend, and I even trusted you

We walked by day and talked by night
And you never took the time to lead me to the light
You let me live to love and to die
… Thinking I would never live on high

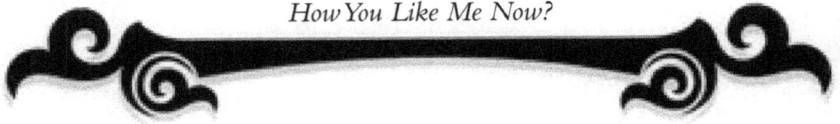

I have learned now, though it may be too late
You could have kept me from this fate
… As I now come up to the end

I know I cannot call you my friend
I will not depend upon you, another person, but I will tell
someone else
Because I have learned to know and love the Lord for myself

4/16/94

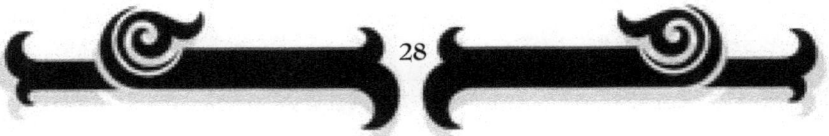

Nanny

I know this to be true … there is a living God
He rules the universe and the sky … For Him that is not
hard
He takes the stars in as He puts the night away
He even brings the sun out slowly, with the break of day
Even though He can put infinity in one grain of sand
He still holds all creatures in the palm of His hand
Yes, roses are red, and violets are blue
This poem, my dear sister, comes special from me to
you
Here's to you, my sister, because you are someone
special to me
May God's blessing be with you, for this day He has
blessed you to see
—Happy Birthday—Nanny

7/12/94

Grateful

The earth is the Lord's and the fullness thereof
He extends to us love, grace, and mercy, all coming
    from above
I ask our Father to open our eyes so we may see
All of our blessings that are to be
I am thankful for all the headaches and all the tears
For the sad days and the fruitless years
To God I give thanks, because now I know
Those were some of the things that helped me grow
We read and learn the Word of God, to hide it deep in
    our heart
When we act upon the Word of God, its truth will never
    depart
Because God will send someone to help us see our
    pride
To teach us true humility and change us on the inside

*Lord, may our needs never come before our need to
     give to You*
*Our heartfelt gratitude and praises for everything You
     do*
*Because true repentance leaves the sin we had loved
     before*
With a strong will to turn from it, and yield to it no more
… You hear me when I call upon You … I know You care
*… For answered prayers, I thank You, Lord, You are
     always there*
*That is why You are all the world to me … my life, my
     joy, my all in all*
*You are my strength, from day to day … without You I
     would fall*

5/8/96

Paul and I as One

*W*hen I look back over my life I really could boast
  About the things that really helped me that most
Sometimes I feel like the Apostle Paul, throughout his life he
went through it all

*E*ven though his life was full of problems and despair
  Bear with me and I will share, in the early days Paul was
not a believer
After becoming an apostle he became a healer
Paul boasted about things that really changed his life
Yet we idolize things that bring us sugar and spice
Paul talked about the time he spent in jail
And his nights on the sea fighting a whale
I can relate to Paul and his incarceration

*E*specially when I look back at my life and see the revelation
  I could boast about the bad things that happened to me
And the peace I felt when I told the Devil to flee
At one time in my life I let many hours tick off the clock
… When I gave my time and money for that ten dollar rock
Even though my life was miserable as hell
I was content during the time I spent in jail

Some people wasted their time worrying about their release
As for me, I love to remember every moment of inner peace
If I must boast, let me boast about what God has done
On how He gave eternal life through His only Son

Yes, the story of Paul strikes even my nerve
Because when we live for the Devil, we get what we de-
serve
Without the Apostle Paul, I could not tell this story
That is why ... to this day ... I give God all the praise, honor,
and glory

9/1/96
—by Kevin Goff

Today

On this day, I will try to live through this day only
Not tackling my whole life's problems at once
On this day, I will try to be happy, realize my happiness
Does not depend on what others do or say, or what happens
Around me. Happiness is a result of being at peace with my-
    self
On this day, I will try to adjust myself to what is, and
Not force everything to adjust to my own desires, I will accept
My family, my friends, my business, my circumstances, as
    they come
On this day, I will do at least one thing I do not want to do
And I will perform a small act of love for my neighbor
On this day, I will not be afraid to be happy; I will enjoy what
    is good, what is beautiful, and what is lovely in life
On this day, I will have a quiet time of meditation, wherein I
    shall think of God, myself, and my neighbor; I shall relax
    and seek truth
On this day, I will accept myself and live to the best of my
    ability
On this day, I choose to believe that I can live this one day

9/1/96

Clayborne Brown, Jr.

The Flight Attendant

"Our First Priority Is the Safety of the Passengers" (D.E.)

When I first started this in the air, home away from home
    career
Like most I said … I would do this six months to a year
Although it cannot be said in a word or two
I now share the role of a Flight Attendant with you
We fly high to places, some far, and some near
… When in the air, we must keep the aisle clear
As we live there may be times of happiness, sadness, and even
    strife
… We meet people daily … some we may never see again in life
We assist the handicap the best way we can
Whether it be woman, child, or even man
Once on board, we help with the luggage and put it away
Yet, we are courteous, wear a smile … and we always have
    something good to say
… We serve snacks, drinks, and even food
And we do everything possible to keep the passengers in a good
    mood
We fly on DC9, DC10, 747, and there are others we fly on too
… The Flight Attendant who strives to give the best service to
    you

1/13/97

35

Here and Now

I have had headaches, and I have shed tears
I have had gloomy days and fruitless years
To thee, oh Lord, I give thanks, because I now know

Those were some of the things that helped me grow
You always let me know that You were there
Because of answered prayers, You showed how much You
care

… Jesus is all the world to me … my life, my joy, my all in all
He is my strength from day to day … without Him I would
fall

Father, open our eyes so we may see
The love, the mercy, and grace that comes from Thee
In faith I pray that You will fill our soul with a love that is
divine

So our heart will be more like Thine
No matter what I do, where I go, I cannot hide
When I need strength, I come to You, my spiritual guide
Even though I know Jesus is coming back to claim the church
as His wife
I know goodness and mercy follow me each day of my life

3/28/97

Obedience

If I gained the world, would I lose my Savior, or would
　　my life be worth living for today?
Would my yearning heart find rest, peace, and comfort
　　in the things that would soon pass away?
When I read my Bible and meditate on what God's
　　Word said
I would learn how to fight temptation from the world
　　and live a life that is spirit-led

There is wisdom to be learned, and there is only one
　　true way to grow
So I humble myself, listen like a child, as I learn what
　　God would have me know
If my path for any reason should be dark on any given
　　day
My faith is in God and by all means I let God have His
　　way

I have enough faith to know the sun will surely shine
And because of His love, He has planned your way and,
　　of course, mine
Yes, God really does have a plan for you and me
When we listen and we are obedient, it will be so easy
　　to see

God is there to help us, guide us, and He is with us
each and every step of the way
Keeping His promise … reminding us daily that His
grace is sufficient for any day
Daily He is working to instill
In our heart and mind His perfect and eternal will
It is said, He will return to judge the world someday
Are you prepared for Him to come, or … are you hop-
ing for a delay?

11/15/97

God's Love

Even though it cannot be said in a line or two
God has blessed me to share these words with you
I have come into the life of Jesus, He is my Lord and
My friend, His power flows though me,
this message I now extend

When you are bold in your witness
by sharing with the lost God's Word
Jesus will honor your service and the lost will be stirred
Because He whose right was heaven's glory
chose to serve here on earth below

Leaving us a clear example of the love He would have us show
God sent His son to die for us, no other life would do
Trust in Christ daily, accept and use the gift He has given you
When your fears seem so large and
you look for proof that God is near

It is then He says: have faith, my child, and do not fear
His love is freely given, yet He supplies our every need
So let's share that love as the spirit leads
… It is a love of caring when the world cries

Because that love is having compassion with Christ-like eyes
There may come a time when things are difficult and you do
not try or show that you care
That is when you should remember that God said,
Love them just as I have loved you and you will bring glory as
My love you share

11/21/97

My Savior

When we see someone suffering, caught in life's despair
The comfort God has given us we must then share
When we respond in saving faith and to the Lord we submit
We then put our lives in His hands to shape as He sees fit

I know I can trust my Savior when I feel the world alarms
Because there is no safer place than His loving arms
I lift my heart to heaven to the loving and kind Father there
Waiting to release comfort in the silent communion of prayer

I am a soldier of the Cross, a flower of the Lamb
I will not fear to own my cross, a child of His I am
Thank you, Father, for Your spirit filling me with Your love and
Your power

Changing me into Christ's image day by day and hour by hour
To share in God's saving truth ... we play a crucial part
Because God is the only one who can transform a person's heart
... Use what God has given you, do not count its worth so small

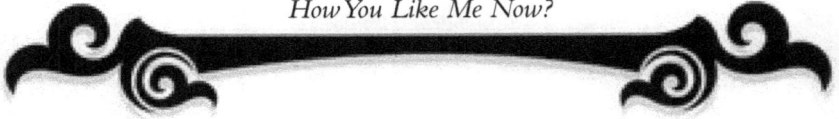

God does not ask great things of you ... faithfulness, that's all
... He is seeking my gold to refine
So I humbly trust Him, because my Savior is Divine

10/13/98

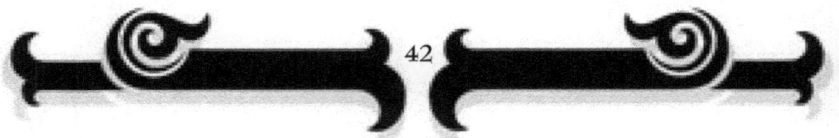

Mountains To Climb

A time will come when you get tired of fighting
Through it all
The more you try, the more you fall
Take time to look at your accomplishments in review
Then you will see they have really been few
You wonder and you ask yourself, why struggle today?
Why not give up? ... that is the easy way
Think of God as a Builder, He has a Master Plan
He made us to be a challenge ... He made man, a man
If the stumbling blocks of life are placed in your way
Think of them as stairways for success every day
... If you really feel like quitting the next time
Don't give up, because God made mountains to climb

3/16/99

Too Blessed To Be Stressed

Refuse to be discouraged and refuse to be stressed
Because when we are despondent our life cannot be
    blessed
When doubt, fear, and worry close the door to faith and
    prayer
There is no room for blessings when you are lost in deep
    despair
Remember when you are troubled with uncertainty and
    doubt
That is when you should tell our Heavenly Father what your
    fear is all about
Unless we seek His guidance when troubled times arise
We are bound to make decisions that are twisted and un-
    wise
But when we view our problems through the eyes of God
    above
Misfortunes turn to blessings and hatred turns to love

                                      3/31/99

A Prayer For You

I said a prayer for you today and I know God must have
heard
I felt the answer in my heart although He never said a
word
I did not ask for wealth or fame … I knew you would
not mind
I asked Him to send treasures from afar, the more lasting
kind
I asked that He would be near you at the start of every
new day
To grant you health and blessings as you go on your way
I asked Him to give you joy and peace in all things, great
and small
But it was His grace I prayed for most of all

3/31/99

A Servant

Even tho' it cannot be said in one line or two
God has blessed me to share another poem with you
I have come into the life of Jesus—He is my Lord and my friend

His power flows through me ... this message I now extend
Lord, help me know from day to day the work I must carry
   through

Grant me the wisdom to discern the things You would have me
   do
I know all things work out for good, because it is in Your design
Yet, You order my steps in Your Word for purposes divine
... It is God's will that we read His Word from day to day

Not just for knowledge, but much more ... to love Him and to
   obey
That is why I walk in faith and no foe or storm will I fear
Because in His Word I am safe and He is always near

Yes, gaining knowledge of God's Word can be a worthy goal
Especially when it leads us to Him so He can nourish the soul
If darkness is around me and earthly joys are flown

God whispers His promise, never to leave me alone
... Physical eyes may not always see the work God is doing
today
But hope in His Word will bear fruit, even though there may be a
delay

One may be blessed with riches and rich in deeds
God wants us to be generous when meeting other people's
needs
Therefore, we should give up sinful pride and take on a servant's
role
Then we will know Christ as a wellspring in the soul

So let's work hard until He comes back and He will reward us
then
Because He promised to return, but we do not know when

11/18/99

Guess What

God formed the world by the power of His word
He speaks to us through the scriptures—His truth is to be heard
If we read the Bible and we are willing to obey
God, by His spirit, will show us the way

Even though I have a caring heart to share God's love to those
    in need
I ask God to help me share what I have through word and deed
Our words are recorded in heaven; therefore, I am careful as to
    what I say

Never using God's name in vain, because I walk with Him day
    by day
I know things of this world will pull at my heart
So I ask God to help me see the end from the start
Children will watch us, and they will imitate things we say and
    do

If they see us imitate the Lord, they will imitate Him too
I ask God to help me see the way through what I'm doing
And give me a faith that is constantly growing

Whenever I am tempted to do something wrong
That is when I need God's power to keep me strong
When I pray, I ask for special strength to keep me true
So I can be straight and right in everything I do

Each day God sends His loving grace to strengthen you and me
… Use today's supply for today and let tomorrow be
Because He has opened our eyes to where our life is going
And we will reap what we have been sowing

12/24/99

Our Love

When two people find with each other new beauty in
    everyday living
They open their hearts to each other by trusting, shar-
    ing, and giving

When two people share with each other a world of con-
    tentment and fun
They know they were meant for each other and two
    people are truly one

It is wonderful having someone to love when the
    weather is sunny and bright
And someone to share life's adventure and joy when
    everything is just right

When you cannot see your way through the problems
    you face no matter how hard you try
Real love comes through on the dark gloomy days
    when the storm clouds take over the sky

Real love makes the rough times less trouble to face
  and every pleasure more fun
Because it brings a peaceful fulfillment that will remain
  through the shadows and sun

When things were not going too smoothly, I remem-
  bered all the good times with you
Because our love held a wonderful strength we could
  count on to carry us through

No matter what happens or what may come to be
I thank God for letting me see the sunshine, because
  you are standing beside me

8/28/02

In This Ministry

Lord, help us submit to You as we follow and obey
Give us the strength to fight the urge to do things our own way

We know Your power can turn a heart from evil, and its
power and sin
Causing one's heart to change while making it new and clean
within

As we hold each other to Your standards and all that Your
truth and love demands
We join our hearts and hands together as we are faithful to
Your commands

Even though You give each of us a task You want us to fulfill
We love to serve You as we attempt to do Your will

Therefore, we make our witness clear as we labor faithfully
So friends and neighbors will turn to Christ from what they
hear and see

If our life is cut short ... our works for Christ will carry on
Because our life of service to the Lord will bear fruit long after
we are gone

12/7/05

Jesus

RISE AND SHINE, O FRIEND OF MINE, LET YOUR FEET HIT THE FLOOR
LET YOUR FIRST STEP BE IN PRAYER BEFORE YOU WALK OUT THE DOOR
EASTER SUNDAY IS COMING, AND HERE'S WHAT I HAVE TO SAY
THANK GOD FOR JESUS CHRIST, BECAUSE HE MADE THE WAY
WHENEVER TIMES SEEM TO FLARE UP, DON'T GIVE UP
JESUS CAME TO EARTH FOR MAN'S SALVATION, AND HE DID DRINK OF THE
BITTER CUP
DAILY WE ARE PUT TO A TEST TO SEE IF WE ARE ON OUR BEST BEHAVIOR
TRUST ME, THE NAME JESUS SIGNIFIES ... SAVIOR

3/28/1994

The Cookie Man

Even though the race is not given to the swift nor the strong
Through God's grace, love, and mercy, I know where I belong
The best friend I've ever had is the one I cannot see
… One I can confide in, because He loves and blesses me

I may not be the strongest or the greatest, my presence may not
    even count at all
When I put my trust in Jesus' power, I know He will never let
    me fall

Yes, the earth is the Lord's and the fullness thereof
I bake pies, cookies, cobblers, all made with a touch of love
Because Jesus is all the world to me, my life, my joy, my all in
    all
He is my strength from day to day, without Him I would fall

Mother

You have a heart that knows every spoken and
　　unspoken need
You have the insight and the wisdom to know when to
　　lead
You have eyes that reflect more joy than your heart
　　could ever find
And arms to hold your child, but never to bind

Even though you are special and a blessing to your
　　family
To your child … mother you will always be
You are a mother with kind and gentle hands
A tender heart that cares and always understands
There is no greater blessing for a child than to have a
　　mother like you

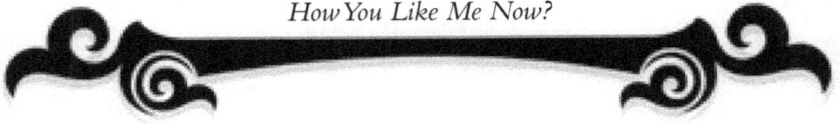

Because you are kind and thoughtful in everything you
   do
You have a smile to share even when things are not
   right
And a godly voice that can soothe, inspire, or even be
   a delight
Here's wishing you life's greatest blessings today,
   tomorrow, and always

Because you are thought about with special love on
   this day of all days
May God's love and peace surround you today and
   throughout the year
Because there is peace and comfort when you are near

Happy Mother's Day

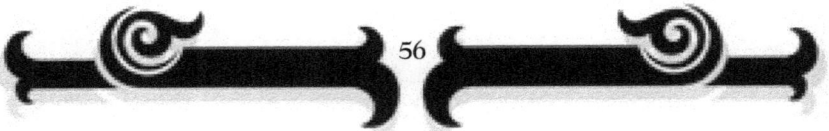

I Love You

If we look at life like a garden and friendship like a flower
We will see its beauty through the sunshine and the shower
Lovely are the blossoms that are treated with great care
By special people who work to make this place more fair
Just like a garden blossoms … friendships grow more and more
    sweet
When worked and tended carefully by someone special we meet
Now, when the sunshine adds its fragrance and the raindrops
    play their part
Joy and sadness add new beauty to life when love comes from
    the heart
… You are still someone special to me
… May God's blessings be with you, because this day He
Has blessed you to see

Happy Birthday

My Lovely

THERE IS NO ONE WHO IS SO THOUGHTFUL, AND OH SO
DEAR
FOR MAKING MY LIFE MORE BRIGHTER WITH LOVE THROUGH-
OUT THE YEAR

MY DEAR LADY, YOU HAVE A SPECIAL TALENT AND YOU
ARE MY DREAM COME TRUE
YOU BEING THE PERSON YOU ARE, I TRULY THANK GOD FOR
YOU
EVEN THOUGH I LIFT MY EYES TO THE HILLS AND I GIVE GOD
ALL THE PRAISE

I KNOW I CAN CONFIDE IN YOU, BECAUSE YOU HAVE UNDER-
STANDING WAYS
… YOU ARE SO THOUGHTFUL, CHEERFUL, LOVING, AND DEAR

YOU ARE THE LIGHT OF MY LOVE THROUGHOUT THE YEAR
MY HEART AND LOVE GOES OUT TO YOU IN A SPECIAL
WAY
… FROM ME TO YOU, BABY …

HAPPY MOTHER'S DAY

A Time To Pray

I got up early one morning … as I went about my way
I had so much to do, I did not take time to pray
Problems came at me and heavier was each task
I wondered, why don't God help me? … He said, you did not
ask
I looked for joy and beauty, but the day went on grey and sleek
I asked myself, why didn't God show me? He answered, you did
not seek
I tried to go into God's presence, I used all the keys on the lock
God said softly, my child, you did not knock
… When I woke up this morning, I paused before I went about
my day
No matter how much I had to accomplish, I took time to pray

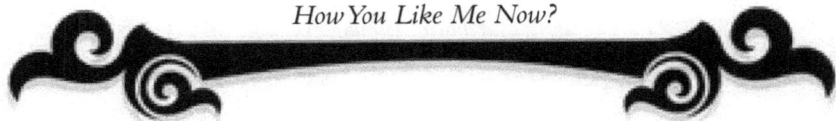

Yesterday and Today

Even though we live in a world that has misery and strife
I truly thank God for being in my life
I once walked along day in and day out
No one to call my own and no one to walk about
Yesterday, I was blind and could not see
Today, I know God walks right beside me
Yesterday, I did not know right from wrong
Today, I truly know where I belong
Yesterday, there were times when I knew not what to do
Today, I know God is there to carry me through
Yesterday, I was shaky, my soul really cried out
Today, I'm happy knowing Jesus is what it's all about
Now, be it God's will I ask that you all pray for me
Because this is a beautiful day God has blessed us to see

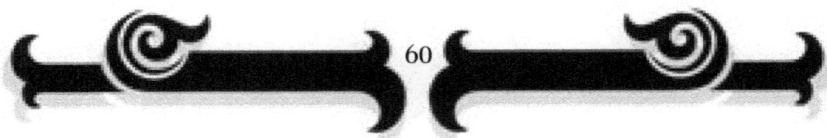